Original title:
Passion and Stability

Copyright © 2024 Swan Charm
All rights reserved.

Author: Eliora Lumiste
ISBN HARDBACK: 978-9916-89-058-5
ISBN PAPERBACK: 978-9916-89-059-2
ISBN EBOOK: 978-9916-89-060-8

United Through Tempests

In the heart of storms, we stand side by side,
Facing the fury, our spirits the guide.
Together we'll weather the fiercest of gales,
Hand in hand, we'll conquer, our strength never fails.

Raindrops may batter, but friendship will bloom,
As lightning strikes bright, dispelling the gloom.
Through thunder's loud roar, we'll sing our own song,
With hearts intertwined, we will always be strong.

The winds may howl wild, trying to push us apart,
But united we shine, as light from the heart.
Each tempest may rise, but we're ready to fight,
In shadows or storms, we'll be each other's light.

So trust in the bond that we've forged through the strife,
With hope as our beacon, we'll cherish this life.
In the depths of the night, our courage will swell,
Together, dear friend, we'll always prevail.

Let the heavens rage on, let the earth quake and bend,
For together, through tempests, we'll rise and transcend.
Though chaos may linger, we'll never lose sight,
United in spirit, we'll conquer the night.

Love's Gentle Anchor

In storms of doubt, you guide my way,
A harbor safe where I can stay.
Your laughter echoes, soft and clear,
With every heartbeat, I hold you near.

Through tidal waves of passing years,
We build our dreams, dispel our fears.
With every whisper, love's sweet sway,
You are my anchor, come what may.

Emotions that Endure

Like roots that ground in fertile earth,
Our souls entwined, for what it's worth.
Through seasons change, we stand so tall,
In joy and sorrow, we embrace it all.

Memories dance like shadows cast,
In every moment, we hold fast.
With every heartbeat, love's refrain,
Through endless trials, we remain.

The Calm After the Flame

When fire flickers, embers glow,
We sit together, warm and slow.
In quiet whispers, dreams unfold,
  A tapestry of stories told.

Through chaos past, the ashes fade,
In gentle silence, hopes are laid.
With every sigh, the night reveals,
A love that binds, a bond that heals.

Unwavering Hearts

Through shifting sands and tides of fate,
Our hearts beat strong, and love won't wait.
In every glance, a promise made,
Together stepping, unafraid.

With hands held tight, we face the night,
In shadows deep, we find our light.
With every challenge, we'll prevail,
Our love, a ship that will not sail.

The Fortress of Us

In shadows deep, we stand as one,
A fortress built, our battles won.
Through storms that rage and whispers soft,
Together we rise, our spirits aloft.

Walls of trust, they guard our dreams,
In silent nights, we forge our beams.
Each stone a story, love's embrace,
In this safe haven, we find our place.

Echoes of laughter fill the halls,
In every corner, love enthralls.
Within these walls, no fear can stay,
The fortress of us, come what may.

Beyond the gates, the world may roar,
But here inside, we seek no more.
Hand in hand, through thick and thin,
In this stronghold, our lives begin.

Eternal Embers

In twilight's glow, the embers dance,
A flicker bright, a fleeting glance.
Within the dark, they softly gleam,
Whispering secrets of a dream.

Each spark a memory frozen still,
A warmth that lingers, a heart to fill.
Through ages past, they light the way,
Guiding us through the endless gray.

When shadows creep and silence falls,
The eternal embers hear our calls.
With every breath, they pulse anew,
Fueling the fire that lives in you.

In the night's embrace, we find our thread,
An ancient bond, eternally fed.
As long as hearts can beat and bleed,
These embers will ignite our need.

Roots Embraced by Time

Beneath the soil, the roots entwine,
In ancient whispers, they intertwine.
Held by the earth, steadfast and true,
Embraced by time, they always grew.

Branches stretch wide, reaching for light,
In search of dreams, they take to flight.
With every storm, they bend but stay,
Holding the past, come what may.

Time leaves its mark on bark and stone,
In lines of age, the wisdom's grown.
Through seasons' change, they stand the test,
Roots intertwined, forever blessed.

From tiny seeds, to towering trees,
In nature's arms, we find our peace.
Through whispers of wind, they play their part,
Connecting souls, heart to heart.

Unseen Chains of Belonging

Invisible links, we feel the pull,
In every heartbeat, the world is full.
Across the miles, a tethered thread,
Binding our spirits, where paths are led.

In laughter shared and tears released,
These unseen chains grant us our feast.
Through trials faced, we stand as one,
Together we rise, never outdone.

A tapestry woven in hues of fate,
Each stitch a moment, we celebrate.
In quiet nights, our bonds reveal,
The strength of love, an endless wheel.

Though distances may stretch and bend,
These chains will hold till journeys end.
In the heart's embrace, we find our truth,
Forever linked, in age and youth.

Love's Steady Current

Like a river flows with grace,
Carrying dreams in warm embrace.
In the stillness, hearts align,
Together we create a sign.

Beneath the stars, we dance at night,
Guided by the moon's soft light.
Hand in hand, we drift as one,
In the twilight, our journey's begun.

Every wave that whispers by,
Echoes laughter, love's soft sigh.
Through the storms, we stand so true,
In love's current, me and you.

With every bend, a story told,
Of moments cherished, hearts of gold.
In the depths, our spirits soar,
Love's steady current, forevermore.

The Confluence of Hearts

When rivers meet, their waters blend,
A fusion rare, where passions fend.
In the merging, vibrant streams,
Life awakens, ignites dreams.

Two souls drawn by fate's design,
A tapestry where colors shine.
In harmony, we find our place,
In every touch, a warm embrace.

The bridges built from trust and care,
In shared moments, we declare.
Each heartbeat sings a sweet refrain,
In love's dance, joy conquers pain.

As seasons shift, our roots grow strong,
Through trials faced, where we belong.
The confluence we celebrate,
Two hearts entwined, it's never late.

A Fortress of Togetherness

In the heart of life's vast sea,
We build our walls, just you and me.
A fortress strong, brick by brick,
Where love's flame burns bright and thick.

With every laugh, our walls stand tall,
In unity, we'll never fall.
Each whispered word, a gentle stone,
This shelter warm, forever home.

Storms may rage and winds may howl,
But in our fort, we shall not cowl.
Embraced in trust, we'll face the night,
In love's fortress, find our light.

Together we rise above our fears,
Through every joy, through all the tears.
A sanctuary where dreams reside,
In this fortress, both side by side.

The Rhythm of Belonging

With every beat, our hearts align,
In perfect sync, like twirling vines.
A melody that flows so sweet,
In harmony, where souls can meet.

The cadence found in laughter's call,
In tender moments, we rise, we fall.
Each gentle sway, a dance so rare,
In this rhythm, we find our air.

Through tempo changes, we still glide,
In every step, there's love and pride.
As seasons shift, we stay in tune,
Together humming a joyful rune.

The world a stage, we take our part,
Two voices blend, a dancing art.
In every heartbeat's gentle song,
We celebrate where we belong.

Boundless Horizons

Beyond the hills, where dreams take flight,
The sky kissed gold, shimmering bright.
Waves of green dance with the breeze,
Whispers of hope, the heart's ease.

Stars at dusk weave tales anew,
Guiding the lost, in night's dew.
Every path leads to the true,
Horizons vast, in shades of blue.

Mountains tower, proud and tall,
Echoing dreams, they call us all.
With every step, our spirits rise,
Chasing the warmth of endless skies.

Rivers flow with stories deep,
Carrying secrets, ours to keep.
Nature's song, a soft embrace,
Boundless horizons, a timeless place.

In every corner, beauty lies,
Magic sparkles in the eyes.
Together we wander, hearts align,
In this vast world, our spirits entwine.

The Tapestry of Commitment

Threads of promise, woven tight,
In colors bold, like stars at night.
Every stitch tells our story true,
A tapestry bright, crafted by two.

Through storms that roar and winds that bite,
Hand in hand, we find the light.
A patterns rich of laughter shared,
In moments tender, love declared.

Each day unfolds a new design,
Layered with care, like aged wine.
Through trials faced and barriers crossed,
In each embrace, we find the lost.

Woven hearts, forever bound,
In this sanctuary, love is found.
Together we rise, through thick and thin,
The tapestry strong, where dreams begin.

Commitment's grace, a timeless art,
Binding our souls, never apart.
In every hue, our legacy stands,
The tapestry crafted by loving hands.

Reflections of a Steadfast Flame

A solitary fire burns bright,
Flickering softly through the night.
Its warmth embraces, melts the cold,
A steadfast flame, with tales untold.

In shadows cast, it dances free,
Whispering secrets to the trees.
Memories flicker, like glowing sparks,
Illuminating dreams in hidden parks.

Through storms it bends, but does not break,
A sign of hope, in every quake.
Its glow ignites the darkest hour,
A symbol of love, a source of power.

In gentle twilight, it softly sighs,
A beacon bright beneath the skies.
Reflections deepen within its frame,
The heart knows well the steadfast flame.

Through the silence, its warmth remains,
A bond unbroken, through joys and pains.
With every flicker, faith reclaims,
In the embrace of a steadfast flame.

Courage in Quietude

In silence deep, where thoughts reside,
Courage blooms, like waves with tide.
The stillness wraps like velvet night,
A whispered hope, a steadfast light.

In trembling heart, a strength unfurled,
Braving shadows that cloak the world.
Each breath a step, each pause a chance,
To face the storm with quiet dance.

Gentle resilience, soft yet strong,
Through whispered doubts, we carry on.
In subtle ways, we find our voice,
Courage born from quiet choice.

Amidst the chaos, inner peace,
In moments still, we find release.
With every heartbeat, fears dissolve,
In courage found, our hearts evolve.

Let the world rush, let tempests roar,
In quietude, we learn to soar.
United in silence, we hold the key,
Courage blooms in serenity.

The Pulse of Place

In shadows cast by ancient trees,
Whispers of history ride the breeze.
Each stone a tale, each path a song,
The heartbeat of this land is strong.

Morning dew on emerald grass,
Memories linger as moments pass.
Sky painted in fiery hues,
Nature's canvas, a bright muse.

Mountains rise like steadfast friends,
Over valleys where the river bends.
The call of birds, a sweet refrain,
Echoes of life, joy and pain.

Seasons shift in vibrant dance,
The pulse of place, a timeless trance.
In every heartbeat, we find our way,
Guided by night and blessed by day.

Love's Unfaltering Journey

In fields of gold, our footsteps trace,
Every glance, a tender embrace.
A silent vow beneath the stars,
To journey together, no matter how far.

Through storms and sun, we hold on tight,
In darkest hours, you are my light.
With every laugh and every sigh,
Our spirits soar, together we fly.

Time may weather, but hearts remain,
In every joy and in every pain.
We carve our story across the skies,
With love's true compass, we shall rise.

Each chapter turns, new dreams ignite,
In the warmth of love, we find our light.
Forever bound, we'll face the night,
With hearts that beat in sync, so bright.

Verses of Vows

Beneath the altar, hearts align,
In whispered words, our souls entwine.
The promises made, pure and true,
In every breath, I cherish you.

Together we stand, hand in hand,
A sacred bond, forever planned.
In laughter's echo and silence deep,
In love's embrace, our secrets keep.

Through trials faced and storms we've braved,
In every moment, love has saved.
We build a life, not just for today,
But for tomorrow, come what may.

As seasons change and years unfold,
In verses of vows, our story told.
With every heartbeat, our dreams will dance,
In this life together, we find our chance.

Harbor of Emotions

In the stillness of the night,
A harbor where dreams take flight.
Waves of joy, tides of grief,
In this place, we find relief.

Sheltered by love's gentle hand,
An anchor in this shifting sand.
With every tear, each smile shared,
A testament to how much we cared.

In warmth of laughter, shadows wane,
Together we dance through joy and pain.
Stories written in trust's embrace,
In this harbor, we've found our place.

From sunrise hope to moonlit sighs,
In the depth of emotions, our spirit flies.
Forever anchored, we face the tide,
In this harbor, love's our guide.

Foundations of Desire

In whispers soft under the moon's glow,
Hearts entwined, a fervent flow.
Dreams awaken, passions ignite,
Together we soar, lost in the night.

Fingers trace where shadows dwell,
In secret glances, love's sweet spell.
Chasing echoes of a distant laugh,
Foundations built on a lover's path.

Promises whispered, a tender vow,
In the garden of hope, we live now.
Time dances gently, a delicate thread,
With every heartbeat, love's story spread.

Sunrise brings a golden hue,
Awakening dreams, both old and new.
With every breath, our souls align,
In the tapestry of love, you are mine.

A Symphony of Steel

Iron clashes in the heart of night,
Forged in fire, a dance of might.
Echoes of strength in every strike,
Harmony found in the chaos alike.

Rhythms of labor, sweat on brow,
Melding passions with each vow.
A world reborn through crafted hands,
A symphony forged, where courage stands.

Melodies rise from the anvil's kiss,
In every note lives labor's bliss.
Against the tide, we carve our name,
In the pulse of steel, we find our flame.

Resilience woven in every beat,
The heart of steel cannot know defeat.
United in purpose, we raise the shield,
In this symphony, our fate is sealed.

Unyielding Affection

Through storms that rage and shadows that fall,
Our love remains, unyielding, tall.
In silent battles, we find our grace,
Together we stand, in every place.

Time may wear, and seasons may change,
But through it all, our hearts remain.
In the warm embrace of a tender hand,
In the quiet moments, we understand.

Every trial, a song we sing,
In laughter and tears, our spirits cling.
Through darker days and sunlit skies,
My heart finds home in your deep eyes.

Like roots entwined beneath the ground,
Our love's foundation, steadfast, profound.
In every heartbeat, a vow we keep,
In unyielding affection, forever deep.

The Dance of Time

With every tick, the moments flow,
In the dance of time, we come to know.
Footsteps echo on life's grand stage,
A fleeting glance, a turning page.

Eons whisper in the breeze,
Lessons learned with gentle ease.
In the shadows, memories play,
Guiding our steps, showing the way.

Seasons shift, as the world unwinds,
In this rhythm, the heart finds.
A waltz of joy, a sigh of pain,
In the dance of time, we break the chain.

With every pause, a breath we take,
In this journey, more memories we make.
Together we move, hand in hand,
In this timeless dance, forever we stand.

The Steady Flame

In the night that seems so cold,
A flicker whispers tales of old.
It dances lightly on the air,
A glowing heart, without a care.

It bravely fights against the dark,
An ember's glow, a timeless spark.
Each heartbeat sings, a steady song,
In its warmth, we all belong.

The shadows deep may try and fold,
Yet here, the light we will uphold.
A guiding force through thick and thin,
Together we will always win.

With every flicker, dreams take flight,
Creating visions, pure and bright.
The steady flame will ever glow,
A promise kept when winds do blow.

So in this life, let fires blaze,
With passion's heat, we'll trust and gaze.
For in the dark, it shines the way,
A steady flame at close of day.

In the Eye of the Storm

Through tempests wild, the winds do howl,
Yet here we stand, beneath the scowl.
In chaos, calm becomes the scene,
A silent peace, where hearts convene.

The world may shake with thunder loud,
And nature's fury forms a shroud.
Yet in the center, stillness reigns,
A quiet space where love remains.

Like a lighthouse on the shore,
A ray of hope, forevermore.
In darkest skies, our spirits rise,
We face the storm, with steady eyes.

The whirlwind's dance may swirl around,
Yet here, a heartbeat, safe and sound.
Within the eye, we find our strength,
Surrounded by love's vast expanse.

So when the storm breaks overhead,
And fear fills hearts with thoughts of dread,
Recall the calm that holds us tight,
In the eye, we find our light.

Intensity in Tranquility

In stillness, depth of life unfolds,
A whispered truth, a story told.
The quiet moments, full of grace,
A soothing balm in time and space.

Yet in the hush, a spark ignites,
With fervor locked in gentle sights.
The river flows, both strong and deep,
In calm, a passion stirs from sleep.

Through forests green and mountains high,
In every leaf, a reason why.
The heart, it beats with fervent song,
In tranquility, we all belong.

So breathe the air, rich and alive,
In peaceful moments, hearts will thrive.
Intensity within the still,
Reveals the strength of unseen will.

With each soft breath, we touch the core,
Of life and love, forevermore.
In sacred spaces, spirits play,
Intensity in tranquility, forever sway.

Foundations of Yearning

In every heart, a seed is sown,
A longing deep, a place unknown.
With dreams that rise like morning sun,
Foundations built when day is done.

We search for meaning, find our way,
In whispers soft, our hopes will stay.
Each step we take, our spirits soar,
Yearning deepens, grows for more.

With every heartbeat, love ignites,
In shadows cast by fleeting lights.
Though paths are winding, trails obscure,
Our hearts shall guide, love's flame is pure.

The echoes call from far and wide,
In every tear, a healing tide.
Foundations strong, we rise and bend,
With open arms, on dreams depend.

So let us yearn, let spirits blend,
In love we trust, our journeys mend.
For in this life, with every turn,
We build our dreams, with hearts that yearn.

The Balance of Euphoria

In twilight's glow, we dance so free,
A melody of sweet jubilee.
Moments bloom like flowers rare,
Euphoria shines in the cool night air.

But shadows creep when joy's too bright,
We tread the line 'twixt day and night.
In laughter's echo, we must find,
The tranquil space of hearts aligned.

As vibrant hues begin to fade,
In silence, still, our fears cascades.
Yet hope will rise from depths profound,
In balance, peace can still be found.

So let us cherish every thrill,
With gentle hands, our souls we fill.
For in the ebb, and in the flow,
The balance of life helps us grow.

Anchored in Embrace

In twilight's hue, your warmth I seek,
With every heartbeat, whispers speak.
Wrapped in comfort, we find our grace,
Two souls entwined, an anchored embrace.

Through storms that rattle, we stand tall,
In every rise, we won't let fall.
Your laughter weaves through every night,
A guiding star, my shining light.

With fingers crossed, we face the dawn,
In every breath, a bond reborn.
A tapestry of trust we've sewn,
In dreams and love, we've brightly grown.

So let the world grow wild and vast,
Our roots run deep, our love steadfast.
Anchored firm, through shifting tides,
Together still, where heart abides.

Whispers of Commitment

In quiet moments, our vows take flight,
A tender oath under moon's soft light.
Through whispered dreams, our hearts combine,
In the sacred space where souls entwine.

Promises wrapped in silver hues,
With every breath, a path we choose.
Through time and trials, a bond so dear,
With every heartbeat, I hold you near.

The ink of trust flows through our veins,
In every joy, in every pain.
Together we rise, a steadfast tribe,
Fostering love, where hope can thrive.

Let echoes of our journey sound,
With whispers sweet, our hearts unbound.
In every word, a timeless creed,
Forever yours, in thought and deed.

An Ode to Unyielding Hearts

With hearts ablaze, we chart our course,
Through trials faced, an endless force.
In every glance, the bond ignites,
A beacon bright through darkest nights.

Through winds that howl and waves that crash,
Our love remains, a vibrant splash.
In unity, we find our strength,
A tethered dream that knows no length.

From whispered fears to soaring hopes,
Together strong, we learn to cope.
With every challenge faced as one,
An unyielding love that can't be undone.

The world may shake, but we stand fast,
A steadfast vow, forever cast.
In this sweet dance of give and take,
An ode to hearts that never break.

The Still Waters of Endearment

In the calm embrace of twilight's glow,
Gentle whispers speak, soft and low.
Reflections dance on waters so clear,
Love's sweet promise lingers near.

Ripples of laughter, memories unwind,
Each gentle wave, a heart's aligned.
Echoes of joy in the evening breeze,
Serenity wraps us, moment's freeze.

Beneath the stars, our secrets shared,
In these still waters, our souls laid bare.
A tranquil bond that time can't sever,
Together we drift, now and forever.

Silhouettes of dreams on a silken shore,
Reflecting love, we seek for more.
As the moonlight bathes our calm retreat,
Endearment flows, forever sweet.

Flames that Endure

From ember's glow to roaring fire,
Our hearts ignite with fierce desire.
In the darkest hour, we find our light,
Flames that endure, burning bright.

With every spark, our passions rise,
Unfolding tales beneath the skies.
Even when storms threaten to pour,
We stand united, stronger than before.

The heat of love in every glance,
A dance of souls, a timeless chance.
In the ashes, new dreams take flight,
Together we soar, into the night.

Through trials faced, our spirits gleam,
Fueled by hope, we chase the dream.
Hand in hand, through fire we tread,
In the warmth of love, we are led.

A Symphony of Tenderness

In the quiet hours, sweet notes arise,
A symphony played beneath the skies.
Harmony wrapped in soft embrace,
Each heartbeat echoes love's grace.

Strings of affection, gentle and true,
Melodies woven between me and you.
Whispers of passion, the softest chords,
In this music, our hearts are wards.

Every pause, a moment we share,
In each crescendo, a lingering care.
Together composing life's sweetest song,
In this symphony, we both belong.

Softly we sway to love's sweet refrain,
Together we dance through joy and pain.
In the silence that follows, stillness we find,
Bound by this music, forever entwined.

When Love Stands Still

In the hush of dusk, our moments freeze,
When love stands still, carried by the breeze.
Eyes locked in silence, the world fades away,
Time loses meaning, come what may.

Every heartbeat sings a quiet tune,
Beneath the gaze of a silver moon.
In this stillness, our spirits ignite,
An eternal bond, pure and bright.

The clock may tick, but we won't rush,
In this gentle pause, we find our hush.
With every breath, our souls explore,
When love stands still, we ask for more.

In the tapestry woven by hands divine,
Moments together, intricately entwined.
Here in this calm, our dreams take flight,
When love stands still, it feels so right.

Tethered to Eternity

In the silence of the stars,
Whispers of time intertwine,
Holding dreams both near and far,
Life moves in a fragile line.

Moments etched in silver light,
Breathe the air of endless night,
Threads of fate, they bind us tight,
Tethered souls in shared flight.

Through the echoes of the past,
Memories forever cast,
In the heart, love's shadow vast,
We find peace when storms are passed.

With each heartbeat, we align,
In the realm where spirits shine,
Eternity, your hand in mine,
Together, we define the divine.

As the world around us sways,
In the dance of night and day,
Tethered dreams shall always stay,
Guiding us along the way.

A Dance in Two Hearts

Amidst the glow of twilight stars,
Two hearts beat in timeless space,
Soft melodies strum from afar,
In this moment, we find grace.

With every step, a rhythm springs,
A waltz that only we can hear,
In the hush, the universe sings,
Connected, without trace of fear.

Together, we forge a new path,
In harmony, our spirits twirl,
A tapestry of love and laugh,
As in this dance, we both unfurl.

Breath of whispers fills the night,
Holding close what feels so right,
In the shadows, we find light,
A dance painted in soft moonlight.

Through the years, as seasons change,
Our love grows deep and wide,
In this dance, we feel no range,
Two hearts, forever side by side.

The Unseen Foundation

Beneath the surface, roots entwine,
Where hope and courage gently lie,
Invisible threads that softly bind,
A solid ground where dreams can fly.

In silence, strength begins to bloom,
A quiet force that shapes our way,
Through every challenge, every gloom,
The unseen holds what we cannot say.

Brick by brick, we build our trust,
In the shadows, foundations rise,
A fortress made from love, not rust,
Where hearts can soar and never lie.

Through trials faced and storms endured,
This bedrock stands, both fierce and true,
In hidden depths, our hearts assured,
Together, there's nothing we can't do.

When all seems lost, we'll find our ground,
The unseen will guide our way,
In every heartbeat, love profound,
A foundation strong, come what may.

Through Every Storm

When thunder rolls and shadows creep,
Together, we will face the night,
In moments dark, our hopes can leap,
Hand in hand, we embrace the fight.

Raindrops sing a somber tune,
Yet in their fall, our laughter rings,
Through tempest's roar, beneath the moon,
Love's shelter shields us, gives us wings.

As lightning strikes, we feel the spark,
A fierce reminder of our strength,
In every challenge, in the dark,
We wander forth, a vital length.

Through every trial, hearts stay true,
Our voices strong against the winds,
In unity, there's naught we can't do,
Together, we will write new ends.

Beneath the storm, our spirits rise,
A bond unbroken, firm and bold,
In storms we find our sweetest skies,
Through every battle, love unfolds.

The Bid for Forever

In whispers soft, we cast our dreams,
A timeless bond, or so it seems.
With hearts laid bare beneath the stars,
We reach for love, no matter far.

Promises made in twilight's glow,
In shadows deep, our feelings grow.
With every glance, a tale unfolds,
In sacred trust, our fate we hold.

Through seasons change, we stand as one,
In every storm, our fight begun.
For in this bid, our hearts we stake,
Together still, for love's sweet sake.

Beyond the fears and the unknown,
In faith we build, a place called home.
With every shared and tender sigh,
We etch our names across the sky.

So take my hand, let's brave the night,
With dreams alight, we'll chase the light.
In every heartbeat, we'll discover,
A future bright, our bid for forever.

Paths Woven Together

Two journeys merge beneath the trees,
In gentle winds, we find our ease.
With every step, our stories blend,
A tapestry, we weave, my friend.

Through winding roads, we laugh and cry,
With open hearts, we learn to fly.
In every turn, a chance embraced,
As paths entwined, our fears erased.

In fading light, our shadows dance,
Each moment shared, a cherished chance.
With arms outstretched, we face the day,
Together strong, come what may.

In whispered words, we find our way,
Through valleys low and hills of gray.
As night returns, we hold the thread,
Woven paths where love is bred.

With every heartbeat close and true,
We find the strength to see it through.
A journey blessed, forever stay,
In woven paths, we find our way.

Anchors in a Storm

When thunder roars and skies turn gray,
In chaos, we will find our way.
With hearts like anchors, strong and bold,
Together, we'll brave the raging cold.

In swirling winds, our souls unite,
For in the storm, we find our light.
With every wave that crashes down,
Our bond remains, a sturdy crown.

Through torrid tides and darkest night,
We'll hold each other, fierce and tight.
As lightning strikes, we'll stand our ground,
In every heartbeat, strength is found.

With whispered hopes, we calm the sea,
In quiet moments, just you and me.
As dawn breaks through, the storm will fade,
In love's embrace, our fears invade.

So when the tempests come to call,
We'll face the waves together, tall.
With trust as our steadfast form,
We'll be the anchors in the storm.

The Harmony of Trust

In silence shared, our voices blend,
A melody that has no end.
With every note, our fears take flight,
In harmony, we find our light.

Through echoes soft, our hearts align,
In rhythms pure, our love will shine.
With open hands, we dare to dream,
In trust's embrace, we find our theme.

Each whispered vow, a sacred song,
Together here, where we belong.
With every step, a dance unfolds,
In every glance, a story told.

As seasons change, our tune remains,
In laughter's ring, in joy's refrains.
Through trials faced, in shadows cast,
The harmony of trust will last.

So take my heart and hold it near,
In every note, we see it clear.
With love's sweet sound, we'll ever rust,
In perfect chords, the harmony of trust.

Threads of Hearts

In quiet whispers, souls entwine,
Each heartbeat echoes, soft and fine.
Through trials faced, we stand as one,
Woven together, till day is done.

Beneath the stars, our secrets shared,
A tapestry of love declared.
With every tear, and laugh that sings,
We stitch our dreams with hope's bold wings.

In every moment, threads unfold,
A bond so precious, worth more than gold.
As time flows on, we hold the art,
Forever joined, the threads of hearts.

Through storms we brave, hand in hand,
A gentle promise, a steadfast stand.
The warmth we share, a sacred space,
In life's embrace, love finds its place.

In memories spun, the past remains,
A future bright, through joys and pains.
With every glance, a spark ignites,
In threads of hearts, we find our lights.

Oasis of Serenity

In the stillness, peace we find,
A tranquil haven, heart aligned.
Under the shade of gentle trees,
Whispers of nature, carried by the breeze.

Rippling waters, calm and clear,
Reflections of dreams, drawing near.
With each deep breath, worries dissolve,
In this oasis, we evolve.

The sun dips low, a golden hue,
Painting the sky in shades anew.
Stars awaken, the night unfolds,
In serenity, our heart beholds.

Here moments linger, time stands still,
Every heartbeat, a sacred thrill.
In the embrace of nature's grace,
We find our solace, our sacred space.

As moonlight dances on tranquil streams,
We drift into our peaceful dreams.
In the oasis, love's gentle glow,
Forever cherished, this we know.

The Anchor of Togetherness

In the tempest, we find our ground,
Through rising tides, love's voice resounds.
A sturdy anchor, steadfast and true,
In the stormy seas, I cling to you.

Through every challenge, side by side,
With open hearts, we will abide.
United in purpose, facing the night,
In the darkest hours, we ignite the light.

Memories forged in laughter's sound,
In every moment, our joys abound.
Hand in hand, we face what's near,
In the anchor's grace, we conquer fear.

Seasons change, but we remain,
A bond unbroken, through joy and pain.
With love as our compass, we sail on free,
Together forever, just you and me.

Amidst the chaos, we'll always find,
A haven of peace, where hearts are kind.
In the anchor of love, we stand tall,
Together forever, we'll conquer all.

Horizon of Hope

On the edge where skies meet sea,
Dreams awaken, wild and free.
In twilight's glow, we chase the light,
A horizon bright, dispelling night.

With every dawn, a fresh new start,
A canvas painted with hopeful art.
We rise with courage, shed the past,
In the light of hope, our shadows cast.

The road ahead may twist and turn,
Yet in our hearts, the fire will burn.
With every step, we plant the seeds,
Of brighter days, fulfilling needs.

In whispers soft, the future calls,
A symphony of dreams, as darkness falls.
With open arms, we greet the day,
In the horizon's glow, we find our way.

Together we'll stand, face to the sun,
With every heartbeat, we have just begun.
In the horizon of hope, we'll rise and soar,
Eternally destined for so much more.

Roots in the Soil of Togetherness

In the warmth of shared laughter,
We find a bond that won't break.
Hands intertwined like strong branches,
Together, in every step we take.

Through storms that may come our way,
Our roots dig deep in the ground.
In the face of trials and doubts,
Together, our strength is found.

With every challenge that we face,
Like trees we grow, and we sway.
Nurtured by love and patience,
Together, we'll never fray.

In the garden of our lives,
Each memory, a seed we sow.
Blooming bright in vibrant colors,
Together, our spirit will grow.

As seasons change and years unfold,
We'll stand tall, hand in hand.
In the soil of togetherness,
Forever, together we'll stand.

Rising with Steady Winds

The dawn breaks with golden light,
As we stretch our wings wide.
Each gust lifts us higher still,
With courage as our guide.

Through the clouds our dreams take flight,
With hopes that twist and turn.
Each steady wind upon our backs,
Ignites the fire, we yearn.

With every challenge that appears,
We rise and soar above.
For in the heart of every storm,
There lies our endless love.

Together we embrace the skies,
With spirits bold and free.
Through storms, the winds may try to sway,
Our bond is meant to be.

So let the winds blow fierce and true,
We'll face them, side by side.
In the journey, we have found,
Together, our hearts abide.

The Quiet Tide of Love

Soft whispers in the night,
The gentle waves that kiss the shore.
A rhythmic pulse, a soothing calm,
In love, we're always wanting more.

With every tide, we ebb and flow,
Our hearts a steady beat.
In quiet moments, we find peace,
Together, love's retreat.

As moonlight dances on the sea,
Your gaze brings warmth to me.
In the depths of silence shared,
Together, we are free.

Through starlit skies, we wander far,
With dreams as vast as space.
In the quiet tide of love,
Together, we find our place.

So let the world around us spin,
In harmony, we glide.
In every heartbeat, every sigh,
Together, side by side.

Hearty Bonds

In laughter and in tears, we grow,
Through every joy and strife.
Our bonds, like roots, go deep,
Nurtured by the warmth of life.

With every story told aloud,
Our memories intertwine.
In the tapestry of us,
Each thread a love divine.

Through thick and thin, we stand tall,
Each challenge met with grace.
In the dance of life we share,
Together, we find our place.

The echoes of our laughter ring,
A melody so bright.
In the heart of every moment,
Hearty bonds take flight.

So let's gather, hand in hand,
In this journey, we belong.
With love as our foundation,
Together, we are strong.

Pillars of Affection

In the shadows, love does stand,
Through storms that shake the quiet land.
Hands entwined, we rise and fall,
Pillars strong, we conquer all.

Whispers soft in the evening light,
Guiding hearts through the darkest night.
With every laugh, a bond we share,
A sacred space, beyond compare.

Roots entwined in the ground below,
In times of strife, our love will grow.
Each challenge faced, a chance to thrive,
Together here, we feel alive.

Memories held, like treasures dear,
In every touch, we conquer fear.
Through trials faced and joys we find,
Our love remains, forever entwined.

With every sunrise, hope unfolds,
Stories etched in the heart of gold.
Through laughter's echo, we will see,
The pillars strong, just you and me.

Echoes of Unwavering Care

In quiet moments, your voice remains,
A gentle echo through joy and pains.
Through whispers soft, love's song we sing,
A melody that time shall bring.

In every smile, an unspoken vow,
Promises made through the here and now.
In storms that rage, our hearts will stay,
Together brightening the darkest day.

With hands that heal and eyes that shine,
We weather the world, your heart in mine.
Every challenge, a step we take,
United, strong, with love at stake.

In laughter shared and tears we dry,
Echoes linger, never say goodbye.
For in this bond, we learn to care,
In every moment, a love so rare.

Through seasons changing and miles apart,
Your love forever fills my heart.
In echoes past, the future's glow,
A tapestry of what we know.

The Heart's Stronghold

In the chambers of my soul's embrace,
You are the light, the safest place.
Guarded whispers and tender sighs,
Love abundant, never dies.

With every heartbeat, a story we weave,
In silence shared, we truly believe.
With strength unseen, we will endure,
In the heart's stronghold, love is pure.

Through trials faced, our spirits rise,
In every tear, a bond that ties.
With open arms, we stand as one,
In the dawn of love, we've just begun.

Building dreams from the seeds we sow,
With every glance, our feelings grow.
In laughter played and sorrows shared,
This heart's stronghold, forever cared.

Through rivers deep and skies of gray,
Together, we'll find our way.
In this fortress, love will not fold,
Forever standing, brave and bold.

In the Warmth of Together

In the warmth of your gentle gaze,
I find my peace on stormy days.
With every heartbeat, a soft embrace,
In your arms, I've found my place.

Through laughter shared and moments sweet,
In every stride, our hearts compete.
In the dance of life, hand in hand,
We journey forth, together we stand.

With whispers soft, we chase the light,
Side by side, we face the night.
In every step, a promise glows,
Together here, love only grows.

As seasons turn, we hold our ground,
In every heartbeat, love resound.
With each sunset, a tale anew,
In warmth and comfort, just me and you.

In memories made, through trials we soar,
In the warmth of us, forevermore.
With every dawn, our hearts will tether,
In the beauty of love, we stay together.

A Song of Loyalty

In shadows deep, where trust holds sway,
Through trials faced, we find our way.
With hearts aligned, we stand as one,
Bound by promises, never undone.

Through storms we sail, side by side,
With every challenge, we abide.
In laughter shared and tears we shed,
A loyal bond, no words can thread.

With eyes that shine, like stars at night,
We search for hope, we seek the light.
A symphony of souls, they sing,
In loyalty, our hearts take wing.

As seasons change, like tides they roll,
Our anthem echoes, strong and whole.
Through battles fought and victories won,
In loyalty's embrace, we are one.

With every step, our path defined,
In loyalty, we've intertwined.
Together we'll rise, through thick and thin,
A song of loyalty, forever within.

The Strength of Desire

Within the heart a fire burns bright,
The strength of desire, pure delight.
A fervent wish, a fleeting dream,
With every heartbeat, stirs the stream.

In whispered hopes, we find our way,
Through tangled thoughts, we long to sway.
This force inside, relentless, fierce,
With each embrace, our souls it pierce.

Like rivers flow, our passions rise,
In every glance, our spirits fly.
The strength of desire, a guiding star,
Together, we'll journey near and far.

With every choice, we carve the path,
Through every moment, love and wrath.
In yearning's grasp, we intertwine,
The strength of desire, forever shine.

In twilight's glow, our dreams ignite,
With whispered words, the world feels right.
This bond we share knows no refrain,
The strength of desire, our sweet bane.

Wellspring of Commitment

In quiet hours, love's promise flows,
A wellspring of commitment, this love grows.
Through time's embrace, we find our truth,
A bond unyielding, eternal youth.

With every pledge, we forge the chain,
A tapestry of joys and pain.
In every heartbeat, trust prevails,
A wellspring of love, the heart exhales.

Through valleys deep and mountains high,
We walk together, you and I.
In storms that rage, we find our way,
A wellspring of commitment, here to stay.

With gentle hands and open hearts,
In life's grand dance, we play our parts.
Through laughter shared and tears we shed,
A wellspring of commitment, always said.

In every dawn, our future gleams,
With every kiss, the world redeems.
Together we rise, forevermore,
A wellspring of commitment at our core.

Riding Waves of Emotion

On oceans vast where feelings swell,
We ride the waves, our hearts compel.
With every rise, there comes a fall,
In this wild dance, we heed the call.

With courage strong, we face the tide,
In storms of doubt, we will abide.
Through tempest's roar and gentle breeze,
Riding waves of emotion, we find peace.

In currents deep, our dreams collide,
Through rolling swells, we take the ride.
Together we surf the highs and lows,
Riding waves of emotion, love grows.

With voices raised, we sing our song,
In harmony, where we belong.
Through every crest, through every trough,
Riding waves of emotion, we scoff.

In evening's calm, as stars appear,
We savor moments, holding dear.
On waves we ride, with hearts in flight,
Riding waves of emotion, love's light.

Embracing the Unshakable

In the storm, we stand tall,
Roots deep, never to fall.
Winds may howl, skies may gray,
Yet together, we find our way.

With each challenge, we grow strong,
In the silence, we belong.
Lifting each other through the fray,
Hand in hand, we'll seize the day.

Cracks in the earth, yet we thrive,
In our hearts, the fire alive.
Together we face the unknown,
In this love, we've always grown.

Embracing change, we find grace,
Every struggle, we'll often face.
Trusting in what we can't see,
Unshakable bond, you and me.

As mountains tremble, we'll hold fast,
In the dance of fate, unsurpassed.
With courage, our souls intertwine,
In the journey, forever divine.

Heartbeats in Harmony

In the quiet, two hearts play,
A rhythm found in soft display.
With every pulse, a story starts,
Written gently in our hearts.

Moonlit nights, whispers sweet,
Every moment feels complete.
In the dance of time we sway,
Together, we'll forever stay.

Laughter shared and tears released,
In this bond, we find our peace.
With hands entwined, we find our way,
Through the night and into day.

Songs of love, on winds, we send,
Every journey, we transcend.
Heartbeat by heartbeat, side by side,
In this life, our love won't hide.

Through valleys deep and mountains high,
Together, we'll always try.
With every breath, we sing our vow,
In harmony, we're living now.

Love's Resilient Dance

In shadows cast, we find our light,
Through every struggle, love takes flight.
With grace and strength, we learn to sway,
In love's dance, we find our way.

Through storms that test our gentle hearts,
We weather them, never apart.
With every misstep, we restore,
Finding rhythm, we learn more.

Moments fleeting, yet we hold tight,
In every tear, we find delight.
For in the dance, we find our truth,
Love's timeless weave, forever youth.

Guided by the stars above,
In every twirl, we share our love.
With laughter shared and dreams that glance,
Together, we embrace the chance.

Bound by faith, we take our stance,
Hand in hand, we dare to dance.
In every heartbeat, our love sings,
Resilient, like the hope it brings.

Roots of Desire

Beneath the surface, feelings grow,
In hidden depths, we start to know.
With gentle whispers, dreams ignite,
Awakening desire, pure and bright.

Branches reach towards the sky,
In every risk, we learn to fly.
With open hearts, we dare to delve,
Nurtured by the love we shelve.

The soil rich with memories shared,
A foundation strong that we have bared.
Tendrils twist and roots entwine,
In every touch, our souls align.

Through seasons change, we cultivate,
In every moment, we create.
With patience, we will always find,
Desires rooted, hearts intertwined.

For every challenge, we remain,
In this garden, love's refrain.
With blossoms bold, we face the fire,
Together, we'll embrace desire.

Symphony of the Heartbeat

In quiet rooms where whispers dwell,
The heartbeat sings a gentle spell.
Each pulse a note, a soft refrain,
A rhythm born of joy and pain.

Within the dark, it finds its way,
A song that soars, then fades away.
Like leaves that dance upon the breeze,
The heartbeat's hymn brings hearts to ease.

In fleeting moments time stands still,
Each throb a measure, each beat a thrill.
Together woven, souls aligned,
A symphony by fate defined.

In laughter's joy, in sorrow's sting,
The melody of love takes wing.
With every pulse, a tale unfolds,
A story shared, a warmth that holds.

So let the music never cease,
In heartbeats shared, we find our peace.
A timeless song that we impart,
The symphony, the human heart.

Pillars of Warmth

In twilight's glow, we stand so tall,
Together bound, we rise, we fall.
With open arms and quiet grace,
We shelter dreams, a sacred space.

In storms that howl and winds that fight,
Our steadfast love, a guiding light.
Each word a brick, each hug a beam,
Our hearts a fortress, warm and keen.

Through seasons' change, as time does flow,
We build the strength that helps us grow.
With laughter rich and kindness pure,
Our pillars stand, steadfast and sure.

When shadows creep and doubts arise,
Together we will reach the skies.
In every struggle, every tear,
Our warmth will shine, forever near.

So here we stand, our spirits bold,
In unity, our bond unfolds.
With hands entwined and hearts aglow,
We are the warmth that love can show.

Lanterns in the Fog

Amidst the haze, where shadows play,
We light our paths, come what may.
With lanterns bright, we chase the night,
Each flicker holds a spark of light.

In whispered dreams, the fog will clear,
The glow reveals what we hold dear.
Together guided, hearts ablaze,
Through the mist, we'll find our ways.

As twilight dances with the dawn,
Each lantern glows—a love reborn.
In moments shared, we find our hope,
A guiding light as we elope.

Through winding paths and trials faced,
We'll navigate, with hope embraced.
The fog may linger, yet our flame
Will guide us true, no fear of blame.

So let us walk, hand in hand tight,
Through foggy realms, we'll find our light.
With every step, our hearts will shatter,
For in our love, the fog won't matter.

Mosaic of Devotion

In pieces small, we find our grace,
Each shard a story, each color, a place.
Together crafted, side by side,
A work of art, where love resides.

In joyful hues and shades of blue,
Each moment shared, a vibrant hue.
Through trials faced and laughter shared,
The mosaic blooms, a love declared.

With every touch, we shape the glass,
A testament to how we pass.
Through seasons' flow, our hearts will blend,
A masterpiece that will not end.

In gentle whispers, bonds are made,
Each piece, a promise, never frayed.
With steady hearts, we'll find our way,
A mosaic bright, come what may.

So let us build, together strong,
In every note, a loving song.
For in this art we call our own,
A mosaic of devotion, fully grown.

The Bridge of Souls

Across the misty waters flow,
Where whispers of old spirits glow.
A bridge connects our hearts with grace,
In silence found, we share this space.

With every step, the echoes sing,
Of love and loss, the memories cling.
The sun dips low, a golden hue,
Illuminates the path, anew.

In twilight's calm, our shadows blend,
A journey shared that has no end.
Through trials faced, we've soared and fell,
Together forged, our tale to tell.

The bridge extends, both wide and bright,
Two souls entwined, in radiant light.
No distance can our bond outgrow,
For in this realm, our spirits know.

So hand in hand, we'll find our way,
Through every night, into the day.
As bridges rise and rivers part,
You hold the key to my heart.

Fires of Devotion

In the hearth of longing, flames ignite,
A dance of warmth, chasing the night.
Each spark a promise, glowing bright,
In every heartbeat, pure delight.

We gather close, the shadows tease,
In whispered secrets, hearts find peace.
The fires burn, a living glow,
A testament to love we know.

Through winter's chill and summer's heat,
Our passions flare, a rhythmic beat.
From ashes rise the hopes we share,
In every glance, a silent prayer.

Together we fan the flames of fate,
With every kiss, we celebrate.
The fire's glow, a guiding light,
That warms our souls as day meets night.

So stoke the flames, let embers soar,
In every moment, I love you more.
Through trials faced, our love's the key,
In fires of devotion, we are free.

The Ground Beneath My Heart

In softest soil, our roots entwine,
Where dreams are sown, and stars align.
Each whispered wish, a gentle start,
The grounding force that shapes my heart.

Beneath the sun, we grow and sway,
Through storms we face, we find our way.
With every touch, the earth takes hold,
In warmth and comfort, love unfolds.

The seasons come, the seasons go,
Through winter's chill and summer's glow.
In every change, we plant our seeds,
The ground beneath fulfills our needs.

A tapestry of life we weave,
In harmony, we both believe.
With every step on sacred earth,
I feel the pulse of endless worth.

So here we stand, hand in hand,
Together building our own land.
With love as roots that never part,
You are the ground beneath my heart.

Threads of Affection

In looms of time, our fibers weave,
Threads of affection, never leave.
With every stitch, we bind and sew,
A tapestry of love that grows.

Through vibrant hues, our stories blend,
Each thread a memory, a loyal friend.
In gentle hands, the fabric tight,
Together we create pure light.

The patterns twist, the colors dance,
In life's embrace, we find our chance.
To stitch the moments, bold and bright,
In every heartbeat, day and night.

As ages pass and seasons turn,
The threads remain, our passions burn.
In every knot, a tale is spun,
A testament to two as one.

So weave with me, through time and space,
In every fiber, there's a trace.
Of love that lingers, strong and true,
Threads of affection, me and you.

Dance of the Unfaltering

In twilight's embrace, we sway with grace,
Each heartbeat a rhythm, we find our place.
With every turn, our spirits ignite,
Together we move, through day and night.

The stars bear witness, we twirl and spin,
In the flame of our passion, we are akin.
The world fades away, it's just you and me,
In this dance of love, we're truly free.

Through shadows we glide, unhindered, unbound,
In the silence of night, our souls intertwineound.
With laughter and joy, we leap through the air,
In the dance of the unfaltering, nothing compares.

Each step we take, a promise we make,
In the song of our hearts, no fear can break.
With music that echoes, our dreams underscore,
We'll keep on dancing, forevermore.

So here in this moment, let time stand still,
In the dance of love, we'll always fulfill.
In the light of the moon, as stars start to gleam,
We'll dance through forever, fulfilling our dream.

Sails Set for Forever

With sails unfurled, we brave the wide seas,
Chasing horizons, where dreams dance with ease.
The winds whisper softly, guiding our way,
As adventure awaits, at the break of day.

Under the sun, our spirits take flight,
The waves sing a song, a melody bright.
With courage as compass, we venture afar,
Our hearts set on journeys, like glittering stars.

Through storms we may wander, through calm we will glide,
With the heartbeat of ocean, we sail side by side.
Together we share every rise and each fall,
In the heartbeat of freedom, we answer the call.

As twilight descends, with the stroke of the oars,
Our souls link like anchors, steadfast on shores.
With a promise of journeys, unbroken and true,
Set sails for forever, just me and you.

So let the waves crash, let the tempest roar,
With hearts intertwined, we are ready for more.
In the embrace of the ocean, we'll always endure,
With sails set for forever, our love will be sure.

The Unbreakable Cord

Through miles and through years, our bond holds tight,
An unbreakable cord, in the depths of the night.
In laughter and sorrow, we share every tear,
In echoes of love, you'll always be near.

In silence we speak, with the warmth of a glance,
Our hearts beat in rhythm, forever in dance.
Each moment a stitch in the fabric we weave,
The memories crafted, as long as we breathe.

Like roots of a tree, we flourish and grow,
Through storms and through sunshine, together we flow.
In shadows, in light, in all that we are,
This unbreakable cord, it binds us like stars.

Through trials we weather, through joy we extend,
This bond only strengthens, as time transcends.
In the tapestry woven, our stories unfold,
The love that we nurture, worth more than gold.

So here's to the journey, with you I'll explore,
The unbreakable cord, forever we'll soar.
Through fate's gentle push, as we boldly tread,
With love as our anchor, we will not be led.

Caress of the Eternal Flame

In whispers of night, the firelight glows,
With each ember's dance, our affection grows.
Soft shadows entwined, in a warm embrace,
The caress of the flame, a tender trace.

Through flickers and sighs, our hearts intertwine,
In the warmth of the glow, your soul calls to mine.
As stars watch us closely, we linger in time,
This caress of the eternal, forever sublime.

With laughter like sparks, and dreams taking flight,
We bask in the glow, under the moonlight.
The heat of your gaze, ignites my desire,
In the dance of the flame, we'll never tire.

With whispers of hope and promises made,
Through seasons of change, our love won't fade.
In this cherished moment, let forever claim,
The beauty surrounding this eternal flame.

So let the world witness, this passion we share,
In the caress of the flame, your heart's always there.
With the fire of love, burning bright and true,
In the caress of eternity, it's me and you.

Wildflowers on a Stone Path

Amidst the stones, wildflowers bloom,
Colors vibrant, dispelling gloom.
Whispers of spring in the gentle breeze,
Nature's beauty, my heart's sweet tease.

Sunlight dances on petals bright,
Dewdrops glisten in morning light.
A symphony played by the rustling leaves,
In this moment, the heart believes.

Footsteps follow where wildflowers sway,
Chasing shadows that drift away.
Nature's canvas, a masterpiece drawn,
In the quiet moments before the dawn.

Fragrance carries on the wandering air,
Delicate whispers, sweet and rare.
Each bloom a story, each petal a song,
In wildflower fields where I belong.

As seasons shift, they'll dance and prance,
In twilight's glow, a fleeting chance.
The stone path calls with every stride,
To walk with grace, and beauty beside.

A Love Like Gravity

Your touch, a force that pulls me near,
In your warm gaze, everything's clear.
Like gravity holding stars in place,
Our hearts entwined, a perfect space.

Each whisper felt like the ocean's tide,
In this cosmic dance, we both reside.
Through fleeting moments, the world fades away,
In your embrace, forever I'll stay.

The pull of your heart, a gentle sway,
Guiding my thoughts in a tender fray.
A love that binds like the moon to the earth,
In every heartbeat, there's endless worth.

No distance can break this wondrous force,
We are anchored, riding love's course.
In the silence where our spirits meet,
I find my solace, my love's heartbeat.

As we orbit in this stellar dance,
I hold your heart in a timeless trance.
With every breath, your light I crave,
A love like gravity, wild and brave.

Storms Beneath Calm Seas

In the stillness, a tempest brews,
Hidden depths hold the world's lost blues.
Waves whisper secrets, voices unheard,
Beneath the calm, the heart is stirred.

Serene horizons hide violent dreams,
Churning waters split at the seams.
Ebbing tides, like feelings, sway,
Torrents wait for the light of day.

A ship's journey on tranquil shores,
Navigates paths of unseen roars.
Calm faces mask the raging fight,
In silence, storms brew, day turns to night.

Search for calm in the chaos spun,
Every heartbeat, a thread undone.
Trust the waves and the moon's soft pull,
Even calm seas hide storms so full.

In every whisper, a thunderous roar,
Life's balance weighted on a shore.
Finding peace amid waves that race,
Storms beneath calm seas leave their trace.

Serenade of the Seasons

Spring whispers soft with blossoms bright,
Colors awaken, a pure delight.
Birds take flight on warming air,
Nature's promise, a fresh affair.

Summer blazes with golden rays,
Longer nights, and sunlit days.
Laughter dances in the warm embrace,
Joy abounds in every place.

Autumn's breath, a cooler sigh,
Leaves of fire, in hues they die.
Harvest moons in twilight glow,
A symphony of letting go.

Winter hushes with snowflakes' grace,
Blanketing earth in a silent space.
The world asleep, wrapped up tight,
In the stillness of the night.

Seasons spin in endless rhyme,
Each one cherished, passing time.
Life's serenade, a tender tune,
In nature's embrace, we'll find our boon.

The Core of Devotion

In silent whispers, hearts align,
A bond so deep, we intertwine.
Through trials faced and joys we share,
Our love, a flame, forever rare.

With every promise, trust will grow,
A shelter strong, as rivers flow.
In shadows cast, we find the light,
Unfading vows, a guiding sight.

Through storms and winds, we stand as one,
Our journey long, yet just begun.
In laughter's echo, in sorrow's song,
Together we are, where we belong.

Each moment cherished, memories made,
In devotion's core, we're never swayed.
Hand in hand, as life unfolds,
In every story, love retold.

As years will pass, our roots grow wide,
In every breath, we take with pride.
The core of us, a sacred space,
In devotion's warmth, we find our place.

Navigating Through Chaos

In the storm's eye, we find our way,
Through tangled paths, come what may.
With courage drawn from deep within,
We steer our course, and so begin.

Amidst the noise, we seek the calm,
With every heartbeat, we hold the balm.
Guiding stars in the midnight sky,
Illuminating paths that swell and fly.

The waves may crash, the winds may howl,
Yet in our hearts, a steady growl.
Through doubts and fears, our spirits soar,
Together we'll face, what's at the shore.

In chaos' grip, we vow to stand,
Each other's strength, a steady hand.
With open minds and hearts so true,
We'll navigate this world anew.

When the tempest fades and peace is near,
We'll celebrate what we hold dear.
With love as our compass, we will steer,
Through chaos, together, year by year.

The Safety of Affection

In tender moments, love ignites,
A refuge found in warm delights.
With every glance, a silent pledge,
In affection's arms, we find our edge.

Soft-spoken words like gentle rain,
Wash away the weary pain.
In safe embrace, we shed our fears,
Building trust through laughter and tears.

With every sigh and every touch,
We weave a bond that means so much.
In simple joys and shared embrace,
We find our comfort, a sacred space.

In storms of life, you are my shield,
With you beside me, hope is healed.
With every heartbeat, joy reclaims,
The safety found in love's sweet names.

Together we rise, together we fall,
In affection's glow, we conquer all.
With open hearts and spirits free,
In this warm haven, we shall be.

Unyielding Embrace

In the quiet night, we find our peace,
With every heartbeat, worries cease.
In unyielding embrace, we reside,
Two souls entwined, with love as our guide.

Through rugged paths and winding roads,
We share the burdens and lift the loads.
In the depths of silence, a connection grows,
With strength and warmth, our love bestows.

In tender moments, where time suspends,
We hold each other, as the world bends.
Through whispers soft and kisses sweet,
Our hearts converge in the dark's retreat.

With you, I find my truest self,
In every glance, there's endless wealth.
In this unyielding embrace we find,
A sanctuary where souls unwind.

As seasons change and years drift by,
With steadfast hearts, we'll touch the sky.
In love's embrace, we stand so tall,
Together, forever, we conquer all.

Embers of the Heart

In the quiet night, embers glow,
Soft whispers of feelings we know.
Flickering light in shadows cast,
Reminders of love that forever will last.

Through the ashes, warmth takes flight,
Shining softly, piercing the night.
Every spark a memory shared,
In the depths, our souls laid bare.

Hope rekindles, brave and bold,
In these embers, stories unfold.
A tender touch ignites the flame,
In stillness, we call each other's name.

Hearts entwined, together we stand,
Ashes to embers, hand in hand.
Time may fade, but love remains,
In the glow, true passion gains.

Through the storms, we find our way,
Chasing shadows into the day.
Embers whisper, bright and clear,
In the silence, I feel you near.

Anchored Dreams

In the still of night, dreams take flight,
Anchored deep, far out of sight.
A ship of thoughts in a restless sea,
Charting paths, where spirits roam free.

Stars like beacons, guiding me home,
In shimmering waves, I peacefully roam.
Each desire anchored, held so tight,
In the arms of dreams, I find my light.

Hopeful whispers on the breeze,
Calling me softly, put my heart at ease.
A sanctuary built on trust,
In the world of dreams, it's a must.

Every heartbeat, a wave on the shore,
Reminding me softly, I yearn for more.
Together we sail through clouds of doubt,
In the sea of dreams, we figure it out.

Anchored dreams, forever we chase,
In the twilight, we find our place.
With faith as our compass, we'll never stray,
Together we rise, come what may.

The Rhythm of Roots

In the earth beneath, rhythms arise,
Roots intertwine, under open skies.
Whispers of history, ancient and wise,
Tales of the heart, beneath the guise.

Branches sway gently, bending low,
A dance of life in the warm sun's glow.
Living stories in every groove,
The rhythm of roots, making us move.

Underneath surface, where secrets hide,
Nourished by memories, the winds, our guide.
In the soil of time, we flourish and thrive,
The music of roots, helping us survive.

In harmony swirling, the seasons blend,
Each note a promise, a message to send.
From a single seed, a forest grows strong,
In the rhythm of roots, we all belong.

With every heartbeat, we feel the beat,
The pulse of the earth beneath our feet.
In the dance of roots, we find our song,
Together we flourish, together we belong.

Flames in the Twilight

In the twilight glow, flames dance bright,
Casting shadows, embracing the night.
Whispers of secrets in the glowing hue,
Fires of passion, ancient and new.

Embers flicker in the fading light,
Painting the sky with hopes in flight.
Every spark a wish, glowing with dreams,
In the stillness, nothing seems as it seems.

Heartbeats race as the flames take form,
Lighting the dark, a beautiful storm.
In the hush of dusk, our spirits intertwine,
As we gather warmth, you're endlessly mine.

Starlit skies breathe life in the dark,
Each flame a journey, igniting a spark.
In the twilight, our souls take flight,
Bound by the warmth, holding on tight.

Together we burn, bright and bold,
In the twilight's embrace, we unfold.
Flames in the night, never to dim,
In the heart of the moment, we learn to swim.

Waves of Dedication

In the morning light we stand,
Casting dreams into the sand.
With each tide that rolls in bold,
Our promises, together told.

The ocean sings our heart's pure song,
Where the brave and true belong.
In every wave we find our place,
A dance of love, a warm embrace.

Through storms that shake and winds that cry,
We hold on tight, we aim for the sky.
Each challenge faced with steady grace,
For in your heart, I've found my space.

And when the sun begins to set,
I'll cherish dreams we can't forget.
For in the silence, I will hear,
The whispers of you always near.

Together we make our stand,
In this vast, unyielding land.
Forever strong, come what may,
In waves of love, we'll find our way.

Seasons of the Heart

In spring, your laughter blooms so bright,
Each moment shared a pure delight.
As petals swirl in gentle air,
I'm wrapped within your loving care.

Through summer nights, our passions soar,
The warmth of love, I can't ignore.
Beneath the stars, we dream and play,
Together we will find our way.

As autumn leaves begin to fall,
I hear the whispers, nature's call.
With every change, our bond grows strong,
In every note, our hearts belong.

In winter's chill, we find our peace,
Two souls entwined, our joys increase.
With cozy nights by fireside glow,
Our love's a flame that will not slow.

Through every season, hand in hand,
In this sweet journey, we will stand.
For in the cycle, pure and true,
My heart's forever home is you.

Balancing on the Edge of Love

On the edge where dreams collide,
We dance upon this fragile tide.
With each step, our spirits rise,
A leap of faith beneath the skies.

In the thrill of risks we take,
We find the paths our hearts will make.
Together balanced, hearts aflame,
In love's brave game, we'll stake our claim.

With every glance, a silent vow,
To cherish this moment, here and now.
The world below may seem so wide,
But with you close, I feel the stride.

When fears arise and doubts ensue,
Your steady hand guides me anew.
In this ballet, fierce yet sweet,
We find the rhythm, the perfect beat.

For on this edge, our souls align,
With every heartbeat, you are mine.
Together, bold as stars above,
We'll soar in flight, our edge of love.

The Solid Embrace

In your arms, I find my home,
With every heartbeat, I won't roam.
A sanctuary, warm and tight,
In your embrace, the world feels right.

With gentle strength, we stand as one,
Two beating hearts beneath the sun.
In every hug, the worries cease,
A precious moment, love's release.

When shadows fall and days are long,
Your solid touch is where I'm strong.
A lighthouse guiding through the storm,
Your hold, my heart's forever warm.

In laughter shared, in tears also,
With every step, our love will grow.
Together facing all that's real,
In your embrace, I always heal.

For trust is built in every sigh,
A bond that nothing can deny.
In the solid truth of every space,
I find my strength in your embrace.

The Strength of Gentle Ties

In silent moments, hearts entwine,
Soft bonds of love, so pure, divine.
Together we rise, hand in hand,
Through storms that threaten to tear the land.

With whispers shared in twilight's grace,
We find our strength, we find our place.
In laughter's glow and tears that fall,
We stand united, through it all.

Each gentle touch, a steadfast guide,
Through all the tides, we will abide.
In every challenge, every strife,
Our gentle ties breathe love to life.

When shadows linger, and doubts arise,
We'll face the dark with hopeful eyes.
For every bond, a story told,
In simple acts, our hearts behold.

So let us cherish, let us hold,
The strength of ties that will not fold.
For in these moments, strong and true,
The gentle strength will see us through.

Whispers of Resilience

In the quiet, whispers flow,
Of strength that lies beneath the glow.
Through trials faced, we find our way,
In every night, there comes the day.

The mountains rise, but so do we,
With roots that dig down deep and free.
A spirit forged in fires bright,
We carry hope into the night.

Each setback met with steadfast grace,
In every fall, we find our place.
With every step, resilience sings,
In the heart of those who dare to dream.

With gentle courage, seeds of change,
We grow, we shift, we rearrange.
The whispers call from deep within,
A silent strength that longs to win.

So let us rise, our spirits high,
Embrace the challenge, touch the sky.
For in each whisper, we become,
The resilient hearts, forever home.

In the Shadow of Giants

In shadows cast by those we admire,
We strive to reach, we dream, aspire.
The legacy they leave behind,
Inspires courage, hearts aligned.

Each step we take, though small it seems,
Is met with hope, ignited dreams.
With giants' strength, we pave our way,
In every night, we seek the day.

We carry forth their whispered lore,
In every challenge, we explore.
From lessons learned in trials faced,
The shadows teach us, hearts embraced.

So let us ponder, let us see,
The path forged strong by those who lead.
In every struggle, every fight,
We rise together, seeking light.

For in the shadow, we shall grow,
With giants' strength, our spirits flow.
In unity, we'll find our grace,
And carve our own, our rightful place.

Echoes of Endurance

Through valleys deep and mountains high,
We hear the echoes, hear the sigh.
In every heartbeat, stories flow,
Of battles fought, of seeds we sow.

The paths we've walked, both rough and smooth,
Have shaped our souls, our spirits soothe.
With every challenge that we face,
We gather strength, we find our place.

The echoes call through time and space,
Resilience carved with gentle grace.
In every loss, a lesson lies,
In every win, the spirit flies.

As seasons change and tides will turn,
The flames of hope within us burn.
With every heartbeat, loud and true,
We rise again, our dreams renew.

So let us cherish, let us share,
The echoes soft, the hearts that care.
In endurance lies our victory,
Together we write our history.

The Heart's True North

When the stars begin to glow,
I seek the path I need to go.
In shadows deep, my spirit yearns,
For the light that softly burns.

The compass points where love resides,
In gentle whispers, it abides.
Through storms and calm, I find my way,
Forever in the heart's ballet.

With every step, the truth unfolds,
A journey rich with tales retold.
In every glance, a promise strong,
Together, we will right the wrong.

As seasons change and waters churn,
With unwavering trust, my heart will learn.
In moments shared, all fears dissolve,
And in your eyes, my hopes evolve.

So let the world around us spin,
Our voyage starts where love begins.
With every breath, we're intertwined,
The heart's true north, so sweet, so blind.

Harmony Through the Fire

When tempests rage and trials test,
In chaos found, we seek our rest.
Through flames that dance, our spirits soar,
In unity, we rise once more.

With each spark, a lesson learned,
In every swirl, our passions burned.
Through heat and ash, we'll find our song,
Together, where we both belong.

As embers glow, we share our dreams,
In harmony, our love redeems.
Through trials faced and paths we've crossed,
In love, we find what nothing's lost.

So let the fire teach us grace,
In every challenge, we embrace.
With hearts ablaze, we'll never tire,
A symphony born through the fire.

In every shadow, light will shine,
We'll weave our hopes, your hand in mine.
With every beat, our rhythms bind,
In harmony, true love we find.

The Lantern of Fidelity

In the glow of a flickering light,
Promises whispered, a sacred sight.
With warmth surrounding, shadows bend,
In the stillness, our hearts transcend.

Each moment counted, joys we share,
In faithful bonds, we lay our care.
As lanterns guide through night's embrace,
In your gaze, I find my place.

Through every doubt, your light shines bright,
Igniting hope within the night.
In gentle flickers, trust abounds,
In every silence, love resounds.

As shadows dance in tender grace,
Our spirits merge in time and space.
With every heartbeat, visions blend,
The lantern held, till journeys end.

Together, we face the dusk and dawn,
In unity, forever drawn.
With every step, our souls align,
In the lantern's glow, our hearts combine.

A Garden of Steadfast Love

In a garden where flowers bloom,
Our love unfolds, dispelling gloom.
With every petal, stories grow,
In vibrant hues, our feelings flow.

Through seasons change, the roots run deep,
In tender moments, memories keep.
Amidst the thorns, we find our way,
A steadfast bond that will not sway.

As sunbeams kiss the morning dew,
Our laughter sings the skies so blue.
With every glance, affection thrives,
In this garden, our spirit strives.

Through gentle rains and winds that sigh,
In love's embrace, we learn to fly.
With every bloom, a promise shared,
In this haven, we are spared.

So let the seasons come and go,
In steadfast love, our spirits grow.
With every day, together we weave,
A garden rich where souls believe.

Milton Keynes UK
Ingram Content Group UK Ltd.
UKHW021127021124
450571UK00005B/73